THE #1 HABIT

THE #1 HABIT

MAKE YOUR LIFE EASIER AND REACH YOUR GOALS FASTER

Turk Akbay

The #1 Habit: Make Your Life Easier and Reach Your Goals Faster Copyright © 2020 by Turk Akbay.

Disclaimer:

The author strives to be as accurate and complete as possible in the creation of this book, notwithstanding the fact that the author does not warrant or represent at any time that the contents within are accurate due to the rapidly changing nature of the Internet.

While all attempts have been made to verify information provided in this publication, the Author and the Publisher assume no responsibility and are not liable for errors, omissions, or contrary interpretation of the subject matter herein. The Author and Publisher hereby disclaim any liability, loss or damage incurred as a result of the application and utilization, whether directly or indirectly, of any information, suggestion, advice, or procedure in this book. Any perceived slights of specific persons, peoples, or organizations are unintentional.

In practical advice books, like anything else in life, there are no guarantees of income made. Readers are cautioned to rely on their own judgment about their individual circumstances to act accordingly. Readers are responsible for their own actions, choices, and results. This book is not intended for use as a source of legal, business, accounting or financial advice. All readers are advised to seek the services of competent professionals in legal, business, accounting, and finance field.

Printed in the United States of America

Jones Media Publishing
www.JonesMediaPublishing.com

ISBN: 978-1-945849-97-8 paperback
JMP2020.4

For my wife, Jill.
Your never-ending encouragement is the fuel
my engines run on. Everyone needs someone
like you in their corner.

Contents

Acknowledgements

We are all in this together.

There are too many people who supported, encouraged, and inspired me to become the person who wrote this book. Although your name may not appear here, from the bottom of my soul, I thank you with all of my heart.

I want to acknowledge the people of America. You welcomed me, gave me a place to call home. You provided me with the opportunities to become whoever I wanted to be and then cut me loose, cheering, "Run, Turk, run!"

I want to acknowledge Esther Hicks and the Abraham-Hicks team. Seeing Esther do her thing because she loves doing it, and seeing her team create environments where we get to refuel our batteries and raise our corks to float to new heights is indeed co-creation at its best. I am an Aber forever.

I also want to acknowledge my dog, 7, who bought our home, helped us travel to many beaches, and allowed me to have plenty of time off to write this book, all the while loving me unconditionally. Little boy, you deserve so much more than long walks, food, and belly rubs. You are my prince.

And finally, I want to acknowledge YOU, the reader. If it was not for your asking, this book would have never come to fruition. I am but a vessel who is here to serve you to find your way back to your true nature—God in skin. Thank you for your gaze and attention. You are loved and appreciated here.

Introduction

My goals were not unreasonable. I just wanted to be rich enough to do my own thing, to have a healthy body to enjoy my life, and to have a loving relationship with someone who loved me back. The self-help gurus and every book I read told me all of those things were possible. I could be, do, and have anything I wanted. But for some reason I was nowhere near my goals. Not even close.

If you put a gun to my head and asked me how much money I spent on self-help materials, I could not tell you. I read hundreds of books, I attended too many seminars and workshops to even remember them all. I bought countless cassettes, CDs, DVDs, MP3s. I promise you, I was not just throwing money at my problems and hoping things would change. I was doing all the exercises, I was giving my all. I was a very attentive student: always in the front row, fully engaged, and devouring anything and everything taught to me.

I wrote my goals in "I" statements, in the present tense, and with deadlines, because goals without deadlines are just dreams. I did my incantations because many of the life coaches and self-help gurus told me my mind did not know the difference between what I imagined and what was real.

My positive affirmations were written on Post-it Notes and stuck to every visible surface; I was told that when I see it, I would start believing it.

But.

Every day I saw less educated people reach their goals faster than me. I met people whose lives started out worse than mine making something of themselves. I was employed by people who I would consider dumber than me.

I was all alone, unhappy, and days away from becoming homeless. I had no one to call. I had nowhere to turn. I thought I must be a special kind of loser to be the one exception to the rule of success.

In my head I was yelling at myself for being such a f@#*ing loser. What an idiot! What made me think I could ever become somebody? This is what I deserved. I deserved to be broke, all alone, and small. In my mind

I had all these big dreams and ideas, but outside, I was a nobody. I knew something had to change, but I did not know what and, more importantly, I did not know how. After all, I was actually doing everything I was supposed to do to be successful.

I am happy to report I do not think of myself in those terms any more. In fact, I can honestly say that I am living what I and many others consider to be a dream life.

I no longer have to work for money. I only take on projects I truly want to work on.

I get to work and co-create with only the people I truly want to co-create with.

My wife and I can, on a whim, decide to travel anywhere around the world and stay as long as we want.

If you are reading the introduction to decide whether you want to commit to the entire book, let me share with you what this book contains:

1. Any goal worth pursuing requires action. If you desire anything in your life, whether it is something tangible (e.g., lots of money, an amazing career, a super sexy partner, a luxurious and comfortable lifestyle) or

intangible (e.g., happiness, self-confidence), you must take action. Anyone claiming that you can consistently turn your dreams into reality without taking action is lying to you.

2. Everyone has a belief system, and our every action is always within those belief systems. You, me, your partner, your parents, we all take actions that are within the boundaries of our belief systems. The silent killer of our potential is that our core beliefs were all programmed during early childhood. Essentially, before we knew it, we were accepting beliefs about reality and beliefs about what is possible or impossible for us. The beliefs we accepted at two or three years of age set the limits for what we think is possible for us today. For most people, the beliefs developed in childhood are still active throughout adulthood.

3. Although there is an abundance of bestselling books, seminars, and workshops to tell people they can be, do, and have anything they want, there is actually a shortage of information on *how* to be, do, and have anything you want.

My purpose for this book is to help you make your life easier and reach your goals faster by helping you identify and develop the most important habit first; also, I will teach you how to jointly use your brain and subconscious mind, which will put your success on autopilot. Regardless of how you define it, your success is guaranteed without exception. You are not the exception in the universe.

Even if you have tried and failed before, there is a simple explanation for that, and when you understand the power of the number one habit, you will possess the must-have ingredient for your journey to the success you deserve.

My spiritual teacher, Abraham, often uses the analogy of vacuuming the floor: imagine you need to vacuum a large dirty room; you get your vacuum cleaner out and start moving it all around the room, moving furniture to get every inch of the floor, working very hard to do it perfectly. But, what if you skipped the initial step? What if you did not plug the vacuum into the power source first?

Although you might perform lots of cleaning action, making marks on the carpet and even sweating a bit, if you skip the critical first step, you will not succeed. Skipping the first step is the reason why so many people try hard but give up before ever reaching success.

I decided to write this book to help people like you and me: for the people who want to improve their lives and to manifest a more fulfilling life, who are ready and willing to take control of their lives and destiny, but somehow either do not take action, or take action but for some reason end up running in place.

This book is written in two parts.

Part I of the book begins with the fundamentals. You will learn an easily understood version of how the brain works, the origin of beliefs, and what happens once a belief is formed. I also show you how to easily analyze and clarify your core beliefs and how habits become habits.

I will be the first to admit that sounds a bit nerdy. But life has taught me that understanding the fundamentals is very important. If you are like me, you probably just rolled your eyes. I know that whenever I hear the word fundamentals, the first thought that comes to my mind is "Boring."

I am reminded of the wax on, wax off scene from the movie *Karate Kid*. Mr. Miyagi promises to teach karate to the protagonist, Daniel. But first, Mr. Miyagi makes him wax his fleet of classic cars, followed by Daniel painting Mr. Myagi's fence in a very specific way.

At one point, young and tired, Daniel-san rebels and demands Mr. Miyagi teach him karate and stop wasting his time with painting fences and waxing cars. Then the old, wise teacher demonstrates to Daniel that the way he made him wax the cars and paint the fence is actually the fundamental actions of karate; Daniel was essentially building the muscle memory for successful results, unaware that he was actually learning.

Part II of the book is all about the #1 habit. We are going to apply everything we have learned from Part I of the book. This is the fun part! The application, the how-tos. How to take the information and make it work in the real world. How to take all these ideas from the book and use them in your own life. Essentially, learning the best way to reach your goals with minimum effort and maximum enjoyment.

Although we probably have not met in person yet, the coming pages will clearly show that we have a lot in common. You will recognize I do not have anything you do not have. I did not start my life with any special gifts. On my journey, every time I failed— instead of focusing on what or who to blame—I started taking notes. I allowed failure to inform my next actions, instead of thinking I am a failure.

If you stop right here and get nothing else from this book except the knowledge to start plugging into your power source before taking any action, I consider this brief interaction with you a success. But this book has so much more to offer to the reader who will continue.

I will assume moving forward that you will not simply take all my words at face value but apply only the truths that resonate with you. Use whatever works for you and discard the rest. At least, that is what I would do.

I often start my talks by saying that "I do not have the secret for success, but what I do have is the wisdom I have gained from all the many lessons I have learned throughout my journey." I do not pretend to have any special gifts. I offer my experience with failure and success in life. My wish is to help save time on your journey to success by not only avoiding the many pitfalls along the way but also knowing how to navigate your pitfalls in a way that serves you best. All of this so that you can begin creating a full and satisfying life.

The more successful you are, the more successful we all are. After all, we are all in this together. So let us begin.

What Do Life and Success Even Mean?

> *All people cross the line from childhood to adulthood with a secondhand opinion of who they are. Without any questioning, we take as truth whatever our parents and other influentials have said about us during our childhood, whether these messages are communicated verbally, physically, or silently.*
>
> –Heyward Ewart, **Am I Bad? Recovering from Abuse**

Everyone who seeks to understand life knows deep down that there is more to life than just working to pay bills until we get old and die. We also know that we are more than what we do: our lives are more than just our actions. These are not earth shattering revelations.

But if we all know there is more to life than working for a paycheck, then why do so many do just that? If we feel our lives can be so much better, why do we not take action to reach our goals? What is that invisible hand that holds us back?

The short answer is *programming*.

As babies, even before we were aware of what beliefs were, we accepted a certain belief system, which began forming our reality. Most parents have no idea this programming is taking place and do their best in raising their new baby. But even before we were aware of it, we were conditioned with a set of beliefs by those that raised us—a system of beliefs that formed our operating system. The beliefs put upon us as babies and toddlers formed the basis of our entire belief system. This is true for all of us.

Do not worry; this is not a super boring book analyzing your childhood, nor is it a book to denounce your parents. But it is a book to empower you to live the life you deserve, so we need to establish a starting point.

Let's start with programming and how that shapes your beliefs. Unless there is an external contradiction to alert us, we humans never take the time to analyze our beliefs. Furthermore, most of us do not even know where or how we got certain beliefs.

The Origin of a Belief

You have an experience that matters to you—perhaps you saw or heard something that made sense to you, or you had an experience that left an impact, whether spectacular or horrific, or some emotion in between. At that moment, your brain assigns meaning to that experience. Bam! A belief is formed.

Until that belief is challenged by a new set of information or experiences that you accept as your new reality, the meaning your brain assigned to that belief remains the same.

When we are toddlers, we think and believe our parents know everything. They have all the answers; they can do things we cannot do. They are essentially like gods to us.

Then one day, usually preteen years, we realize they are not gods at all: they are just people.

To a preteen who is learning about her place in the world, parents have all of a sudden become the out-of-touch old people who are trying to ruin her life.

Usually by our twenties, we notice our parents are just people having human experiences like the rest of us. Having had our own run-ins with life, our perspective and how we relate to them shifts. They go from being the gods of our childhood to regular people who are learning from their own life experiences.

We will explore the impact of beliefs in later chapters, but for now, start recognizing your beliefs and how they change based on where you are in your various life stages. When you begin thinking about the validity of your beliefs, you will become aware that some continue to be true and accurate while others no longer serve you and are in need of an update.

Life and the Meaning of Life

Most people view life as segments of linear chunks: a series of days we live, one after another. There was yesterday, there is today, and there is a good chance there will be a tomorrow. I was a baby, then I was a toddler, I became a teenager, now I am an adult. And that is life.

Although these are partially accurate descriptions, viewing our lives in linear terms instead of in layers, denies us the opportunity to extract many lessons and meanings we can gain from our daily experiences.

I once hired a great therapist, Dori. She compared life to a road trip and each of us as drivers of our own bus.

She explained that each part of our being represented different personalities that were passengers on the bus. Each personality has different needs, different perspectives, and each personality wants to be in charge and drive the bus to the destination it prefers. With every decision we make, we decide which personality shows up, which to listen to—which gets to drive the bus.

That analogy resonated with me and reminded me that I am a combination of many different parts. I know I have a hyper-motivated, ready-to-conquer-the-world self as well as a go-hide-in-a-hole-somewhere self. There is the part of me that loves to work out and be healthy, and the other part who wants to eat a whole pizza and binge watch Netflix. They all make up the parts of who I am. Just as my body is composed of different body parts, the multifarious personalities within each of us make up our entire being. When we are aware of these personalities, and what parts they play in our lives, we get to choose who shows up and when.

A successful life is choosing to be the driver of your own bus by being deliberate in which part of yourself steps up and takes control of the wheel. Experiences determine all of this.

What Exactly Is Success Anyway?

We each have our own definition of success and measure everything in our lives based on that definition. When people are asked how they define success, their answers usually include some variation of money, health, family, and self-worth. How you define success in your life has definite consequences on how you live your life. One's initial concept of success is based on the programming we received as children. Most children start creating their fundamental beliefs within the first three years of their lives.

Children quickly learn that when their behavior matches the desires of their parents, they get rewarded, and when they misbehave, they lose the reward and possibly get punished: this is called *operant conditioning*. If you act right, you are part of the group, if you do not, you are in trouble. Naturally, children learn to adopt and accept the beliefs of their parents, willingly or as a result of a desire to survive.

When parents use material wealth to measure the success of life, there is a good chance their children will as well. If the people around you measured success only in financial terms, then there is a good chance you will not feel successful until you have reached a certain level of wealth—even if there are other areas of your life where you are obviously successful. Why not take a few minutes now to think about how you define success in each area of your life. Is your definition of success the same as your family or friends or your spouse or partner? Take the time to choose what success means to you.

Based on my life experience, success is an internal job. If you do not define what success means to you, your life will be a constant chase of an unattainable mirage and will lack true satisfaction.

The late author Steven Covey (1989) teaches in his book *The 7 Habits of Highly Effective People* to "begin with the end in mind." That means defining what a successful outcome looks like before taking any action, regardless of how big or how small the end. For example, before I sat down to write this chapter, I decided that success for today's session is to write for an hour, then take a twenty-minute break and decide if I will continue to write more or call it a day. I am reaching the hour mark. Today's session is a success already. I will celebrate and know I have finished what I set out to do for this part of my day. After my twenty-minute break, I may come back and write, or I may not. But at least I know for sure I achieved success in this part of my day.

If you truly want to be successful in life, you have to decide what that looks like for you. Of course, you can and will be inspired by others, but always keep in mind that only you can decide how to define success. Basing your criteria for success on someone else's measure will never be truly satisfying for you. You must base your measure of success on what is important to you.

While living in Orange County, California, in the late nineties, my best friend from Turkey sent me a gift box of olive oil soaps he was producing back home. The recipe for this amazing soap was over five-hundred years old; the main ingredient was the local olives grown on the Aegean coast of Turkey. It was the most amazing soap you could imagine. The soap was so nourishing to the skin; there was no need to use moisturizers afterwards. Living in Cali, thinking like a Californian dude, I knew this was something I could sell here, making a lot of money for the both of us.

I immediately sent soap samples to large companies in California who sold all-natural products. In less than two weeks one of the buyers called with a twenty-thousand-dollar order. I immediately called my best friend and gave him the great news. To my surprise, he responded that he was not interested.

Shocked, I asked him how much money he made in the previous year? His response: twenty-thousand dollars. On a single sale I made him as much money as he was going to make in one year, yet he was not interested. He said, "You are the one who wants to make money. I prefer to go fishing and enjoy my days."

A successful life for me meant making as much money as I could, but for him it was to have a low-key life and spend his days fishing. There is not a right way or wrong way to measure success; it should always be an internal process.

One of the biggest causes of stress in our lives is that we do not usually question who we really are: the difference between who we *think* we are and who we actually are.

While in Bali, Indonesia, in 1998, a monk shared with me a parable that helped expand my perspective on how I experience life. The story was about six blind monks and the elephant. Six blind monks heard about an elephant and wished to know what an elephant was like. They were asked to describe the animal after touching it.

The first blind monk put out his hand and touched the side of the elephant: "How solid! An elephant is like a wall." The second blind monk put out his hand and touched the trunk of the elephant: "How round! An elephant is like a snake." The third blind monk put out his hand and touched the tusk of the elephant: "How sharp! An elephant is like a spear." The fourth blind monk put out his hand and touched the leg of the elephant: "How tall! An elephant is like a tree." The fifth blind monk reached out his hand and touched the ear of the elephant: "How wide! An elephant is like a fan." The sixth blind monk put out his hand and touched the tail the elephant: "How thin! An elephant is like a rope."

They all argued over the correct description of the beast, all sticking to their own experience.

A wise sage happened to hear the argument, stopped and asked the monks, "What is the matter?" They said, "We cannot agree on what the elephant is like." The wise sage then calmly said, "Each one of you is correct, and each one of you is wrong because each one of you has only touched a part of the elephant's body. Thus, you only have a partial view of the animal. If you put your partial views together, you will get an idea of what an elephant looks like."

This old story can help us understand how to perceive our total self.

When you look in a mirror and see your reflection and say, "That's me," you are only partially correct. Because the whole you is so much more than just your physical body. The whole you is the combination of your body, your subconscious mind, all your personalities, and all the lessons you have learned from your life experiences. Believing the body you see with your eyes in the mirror is your entirety is just like holding the tail of an elephant and saying the elephant is like a rope.

CHAPTER 2:

WHO DO YOU THINK YOU ARE: THE MIND OR THE BRAIN?

How can a three-pound mass of jelly that you can hold in your palm imagine angels, contemplate the meaning of infinity, and even question its own place in the cosmos? Especially awe inspiring is the fact that any single brain, including yours, is made up of atoms that were forged in the hearts of countless, far-flung stars billions of years ago. These particles drifted for eons and light-years until gravity and change brought them together here, now.

–V.S. Ramachandran, *The Tell-Tale Brain: A Neuroscientist's Quest for What Makes Us Human*

We are confused about who we are as a whole because human babies rely entirely on others for survival. Newborn humans have absolutely no protection against nature: they cannot walk for nearly a year or support their heads for several months after birth. Our survival is 100 percent dependent on conforming to a preexisting set of dynamics. Before you even began to walk or say your first words, you genetically knew that without the support of the bigger, stronger humans, you could not survive. So if you wanted to survive, you had to conform to their standards and be accepted by them.

Let's remove the attachments and look at humans in mechanical terms. We humans are a combination of three parts:

1. the brain (the hard drive, the smartphone)
2. the subconscious mind (the operating system)
3. the consciousness (the person who is using the smartphone)

Let's start with your brain: the smartest device in the entire universe. The human brain is amazing and so complex that not even experts who study the brain fully understand how it works. So, we are going to stay super general.

The brain is designed not only to think but also to analyze information received by your five senses. (If you ever want to remind yourself that the brain is amazing, remember you never have to inform your body to heal your own cuts and bruises.) Our brains are how we (our consciousness) relate to the physical world. Your brain runs every activity you do with your physical body, from swiping left with your index finger to throwing up when you drink old milk.

The brain is a tool designed to think, and it does this constantly. If you are awake, your brain is thinking. Not just thinking but also learning and recognizing patterns. Even as you are reading these words your brain is hearing all the ambient noises and analyzing them without conscious effort. Imagine for a minute what would happen if you heard a huge crash right now: your brain would immediately analyze that sound and run it against all the other similar crashing noises to figure out if that was a car crash outside of your house, if a tree had fallen on your roof, or if a cabinet full of dishes just shattered. And you would react differently to each of those scenarios.

Your brain runs through similar scenarios hundreds of times a day, all in the background without you ever recognizing it. All day, every day. Something also worth remembering is that your brain's learning potential is unlimited. As long as you are willing to think, you can literally learn anything you want to learn.

But just as your smartphone will not work without an operating system, your brain cannot work without its own operating system. The operating system for your brain is your subconscious mind.

When starting a smart device, there is a slight delay from the time you turn it on to when you can start using it. That delay is the waking up of the operating system. Before any other function is available on the device, the operating system has to launch and wake up the rest of the programs. Those of you who are not trained in the computer world may not necessarily know exactly how the operating system works because it runs quietly in the background below all the other applications we use. Without an operating system, your smartphone becomes just a paperweight.

The subconscious runs in the background. Without your subconscious mind, you would be like a mannequin in a store window. We usually do not notice it because the subconscious mind is quiet and works in the background. It is not a feature of the brain but, in fact, is the superstar hiding behind the curtain. Our subconscious mind is a thousand times more powerful than our brain. The subconscious mind can process things much faster and is not bound by the limitations of the five senses like our brain. It is capable of making connections we cannot fully grasp. If your brain was a smart phone, your subconscious mind would be a quantum computer. That is why it is in charge of the most vital functions like our organs and our breathing.

You may use your brain and willpower to move your physical body, but you cannot will your stomach to stop digesting for even half a second, no matter how hard you try.

The subconscious mind is also in charge of your sympathetic nervous system, which controls the fight or flight response. If you were to step off the curb and see a fast approaching car, you would not contemplate and calculate, you would just react. All the calculations are done by your subconscious mind. But, how does your subconscious know what to do?

Think of your subconscious mind as a large memory bank where everything your brain has observed and processed over all the years of your life is stored. Every bit of information your brain has analyzed since the moment of your birth is in your subconscious mind. Everything you have seen with your eyes, heard with your ears, tasted with your tongue, touched with your skin, and every idea you have ever thought is filed and stored in your subconscious mind. And it is all available for your supercomputer brain to access.

Have you ever overslept on the day of an important meeting? You may have noticed how quickly you were able to get up, shower, get ready, and be out the door in a fraction of the time it usually takes you on other days. That is the power of your subconscious mind.

So, if our subconscious mind is so smart and contains our life's information, why can we not access the entirety of that information? This question brings us to the third—and most relevant—part of your whole being: your consciousness.

What is consciousness? It is the eternal part of you: the decision-maker inside your head. You have most likely heard people refer to their body as a temple. Your consciousness is what resides in that temple. Any time you are contemplating a decision, whether what to eat for dinner or if you should take that job in another state, there is always an internal discussion that happens inside your head before you start talking with others.

Like a courtroom where one side argues for one decision while the other side for another, the conscious part decides and declares, "This is what I'm going to do."

If you remember the bus analogy from chapter one, your consciousness is the one who decides who will be driving the bus. It is the part that decides on the "meaning" of things, including these words.

Our consciousness is how we relate to the entire universe. Scientists have been trying to figure out what consciousness is since the beginning of its study. You now know the reasoning behind this. Consciousness cannot be explained through the five senses. It is the subjective part of our being and it is very personal to each and every one of us. I think of consciousness as the being behind all the masks we wear.

When we talk about our being, we usually are referring to consciousness. Do you remember my saying you can be, do, and have anything you want from the introduction? The being in that sentence is referring to consciousness. Any time you are inspired, all parts of your whole being are aligned perfectly.

So, in a nutshell, the real you is the sum of your brain, your subconscious mind, and your consciousness. Just like your hands, your organs and your brain are all different parts of your body and each part contributes to the whole. Your subconscious mind and the lessons you have learned along the way all contribute to who you are as a whole being. So with each lesson you learn in life, you are forever changing, forever evolving.

Because we all relate to our external world through our five senses, we humans collectively mistook and accepted what we see, hear, smell, taste, and touch as "reality." We continued this narrative from generation to generation with the raising of our children. But that is not the whole picture. At best, what many call reality is shorthand for what is "tangible."

Over the years we are conditioned to accept ourselves as only what we can see in the mirror. The idea is not that your body is not you but that you are more than your tangible body. By understanding the multiple parts of your being and learning to use them for which they are designed, you will increase the speed of your success in every area of your life.

When we stop only using our brains to run the show and start adding our subconscious mind to the mix, we have access to so much more information than we realize. We gain access to all the lessons we have learned along the way. Additionally, when you add your consciousness to the mix, you become invincible. Anyone who meditates regularly can support this truth. When we quiet our minds and stop our brains from running amok, even for a few minutes, a whole new world opens up and we get access to so much more.

Use your brain to think, use your subconscious mind to guide and produce ideas, and use your body to act on those ideas. You will absolutely reach any goal you set for yourself, regardless of how impossible you think it is right now. You absolutely will have access to anything and everything you will ever need.

I spent quite a long time studying efficiency and how to get the best results with minimum effort. I discovered that the best return on investment are habits. Habits essentially allow you to put your life on autopilot. Obviously, you have figured out from the title of this book that the #1 habit will guarantee your success. But let's first cover what habits are.

CHAPTER 3:

HOW TO EASILY CREATE NEW HABITS

Your thoughts become your words,

Your words become your actions,

Your actions become your habits,

Your habits become your values,

Your values become your destiny.

–Gandhi

American Heritage Dictionary of the English Language defines a *habit* as "a recurrent, often unconscious pattern of behavior that is acquired through frequent repetition." Habits are shortcuts our brain creates to save time and energy. Habits are like when we call a preprogrammed name in our phones. I press the name of the person, and my phone dials the entire ten digits and completes the call. The details of habitual behavior often go unnoticed. When an action is a habit, you do not think about what you are doing: it just gets done.

I know when I need to call my wife, I press the top number on my favorites list and my phone does all the dialing.

How often have you driven to a destination without noticing the details of the drive? Happy the work day is over, you may remember starting the ignition, but before you know it, you are home without even noticing how you got there. Compare how effortlessly you maneuver through the roadways today to the first few months you began driving. I know I was nervous. My heart was pounding hard, my hands grasping the steering wheel in a death grip. I was trying to remember everything at the same time. I was attentively driving the speed limit, but I felt like all the cars were driving way too fast, coming right at me. But now, I do not even give a second thought to driving. I hop in my car, turn on my favorite music, and head on my way. What changed? To put it simply, driving a car became a habit. Driving is just one of the thousands of habits my brain has created.

Since there is no shortage of books, seminars, and YouTube videos on the best way to create new habits, I will not get into the details here. But I do want to share the following three points:

1. When something becomes a habit, you never have to "think" about it again. You probably do not remember it, but when you were a toddler and first learning to put your shoes on by yourself, you had a fifty-fifty chance of getting it right. Chances are, a time or two, you attempted to proudly walk out of the house with your shoes on the wrong feet until an adult close by noticed and helped you out. But now that you have mastered the art of putting on your shoes, there is zero chance of doing it wrong. Since learning to tie your shoes as a little kid, you have never had to stop and think about how to do this. It has become a habit.

2. Your brain automatically turns any behavior you repeat into a habit to free up space and save energy. You probably are not aware of many things you habitually do each and every day. But once you understand and accept this fact, you can consciously create the habits you want, just like the thousands of habits your brain created unconsciously.

3. Our mental attitudes and the way we use our brains to think are also habits. You, me, and everyone we know think about things in a habitual way. When you are around the same people regularly, you begin recognizing the repetitive themes of their stories. Because we have habitual ways of looking at the world, they may be talking about different subjects, but their

perspective and the pictures they describe are pretty much the same.

Our brain's ability to form habits was essential to the human race's development from hiding in caves, with survival as the sole purpose, to maneuvering to the top of the food chain. Without our cognitive resources, we humans would have no way to survive in nature. We do not have furs to keep us warm, shells to protect us, or claws and sharp teeth to kill things. Human offspring are totally dependent, for many years, on other humans for staying alive. But we do have the ability to mimic what we experience, and our brains have a natural tendency to create habits.

Once a habit is formed, it frees up energy and space in our brain, no longer needing to focus on that habituated activity. This allows us to learn and focus on something new, eventually creating another habit. Our prehistoric ancestors, who shaped stones into spears, did not have meetings and instructions on how to make weapons to survive; they mimicked one another. When they repetitively did the same thing, their brains formed these actions into habits. Once the action became a habitual activity, they were able to make improvements, which then freed up more and more brain power for new ideas.

The way we think and how we frame our feelings are also habits. It is essentially a loop playing over and over again in our heads. Just like you've habituated shoe tying and driving, how you think about yourself and how you feel about your self-worth is also on a loop. You pretty much think about the same things you thought about yesterday, and yesterday you were thinking about the same things you were thinking the day before. Over 90 percent of the thoughts we think each day are the same. That can be scary if what you are thinking is not what you actually want in life. But this is what makes our brains happy: being able to form habits to keep things simple and conserve energy.

Before we get to how to change these loops (i.e., form new habits), I want to insert one critical point: the way you think about yourself today is directly impacted and shaped by the family and friends you had during the first four years of your life. This is a fact generally accepted by everyone who has studied early child development.

Take a moment now to think about the first four years of your life. What year was it? What was happening in the world? What was happening in the country where you lived? How old were your parents? Where were they in their own lives? Were they equipped to have a baby? Was there the talk of need when you were a baby or did your parents have an abundance mindset? What possible beliefs do you think your brain accepted before building habits around it?

The purpose of thinking about our toddler years is to provide a starting point for understanding the conditions in which our subconscious minds were being programmed and recognizing the beliefs our brains were exposed to when it was creating unconscious habits. We use this information to generate acceptance with compassion rather than using it to rationalize the way we are at the present time.

Like it or not, our brains are habit building machines. Always working to identify repeated actions and patterns and turning them into habits. If you start paying attention to your thoughts, you will notice 99 percent of the thoughts you think today are similar to what you thought yesterday. Because your brain likes predictability and aims to save brain power, your brain will jump right back on to yesterday's thoughts and continue where it left off. It is your brain's way of rebooting, making sure all the loops are running, keeping the same theme active. Whenever your brain comes across a new piece of information, it treats it as a threat to its normal way of doing things.

New ways of being threaten the status quo: many people report feeling anxiety just thinking about a new business idea, relocating to a new city, or having a baby. When our brains do not have an existing reference for a subject, it triggers the feeling of fear, just in case you need to run away. If you have ever felt fear about something new, even when there is no actual threat, going against entrenched habits is the reason for it. Your brain is trying to protect you from yourself. To shift this, you must create the habit of consciously directing your brain to think new thoughts, starting upon waking in the morning. This conscious directedness allows you to be in charge of your thinking, instead of the old programming of years past.

Once you understand and accept your brain loves to think, and it is always thinking the same thoughts again and again, you can put this knowledge to good use. By consciously guiding your brain to think the thoughts in the direction of where you want to build habits, you can "hack" your brain into replacing the habitual thoughts that were programmed in your childhood with the ones that best serve you today. Building new habits is super easy when you know how to use your brain.

The following is the process for building new habits:

1. Decide on the new outcome you want to create. As we know from earlier, when changing a habit, expect a fear response from your brain. Because of this, it is better to start with easy things and single step processes so that your brain can become familiar with habit-changing. For example, let's say you have a messy house/desk/car. The new outcome you want is to be a neater person. Declare and own the new behavior! If you want to be a neat person, the action associated with that is putting things where they belong. This is an important step for your brain to easily connect the habit and action you are forming. So the declaration you must think is "I am a neat person. I always put things where they belong."

2. Consciously take those actions. Remember your brain is looking for patterns to turn them into habits. So do not wait for occasions, but create your own occasions. Consciously think, "I just brushed my teeth. I will put my toothbrush where it belongs. I'll also put the toothpaste where it belongs." After making coffee, say and put your coffee cup where it belongs. It sounds so easy but can be challenging when we meet the resistance given by our old, messy habits. It takes a conscious effort to create new habits, but once you learn, it is just like riding a bike.

In just a few days of you holding your brain to the new thought pattern, your brain will automatically start building the desired habit. Super easy and very effective. There is no limit to your brain's learning capacity, and there is no limit to your potential either. If you do not agree with that statement, it is because you have a habit of believing you are not worthy. The good news is that you can change that belief just by using the three steps above.

Just like learning to ride a bicycle, once you learn this sequence and commit to routine practice, there is absolutely nothing you cannot turn into a habit. Can you create new habits to earn more money? Yes! Can you create new habits to be a better spouse? Yes! Can you create new habits to be a happier person? Absolutely! There is literally no limit to your habit building potential.

When I was doing research for this book, I was excited to come across quite a few self-help books on the subject of habits. As you can see from this chapter, building good habits is the most efficient way to reach your goals. I know from experience that once you start building habits consciously, you will maximize your gains with minimal effort.

Speaking of efficiency and maximizing your gains, there is one habit, if you build before all the others, that will improve every part of your life as well as the lives of all the people around you. I know this not just from my own experience but from every person I have worked with. Everyone who has ever tried it agrees that when you work on the #1 habit first, it makes everything else easier. I wrote this book: to inform the world about this fundamental habit: your mental attitude.

We are now done with the fundamentals. You know everything necessary to take your game to the next level!

THE MISSING LINK TO TRUE SATISFACTION

Nothing can stop the man with the right mental attitude from achieving his goal; nothing on earth can help the man with the wrong mental attitude.

–Thomas Jefferson

After reviewing the fundamentals, you are now ready to jump in and take your game to the next level. You are now aware that everything you have created in your life so far—the good, the bad, and the ugly, without exception—has been the combination of how you have used your brain, what your subconscious believes, and your habits. We covered how each of your actions is based on what you think. Regardless of the manifestations you want to bring into your life, the easiest and the most efficient way to guarantee success is by consciously creating habits. By building good habits, the things you want will come to you automatically. Let's start with the number one habit, which most people do not even recognize as a habit: your mental attitude.

True satisfaction in life comes from having dreams and going after those dreams. So if you want to reach your dreams with ease, the first habit you must develop is a positive mental attitude. It is not enough to claim that you are an optimist: you must consciously practice the habit of directing your mental attitude to think positively. Looking for what is right and what the lessons are to learn in all situations will enable you to take actions aligned with your goals and make your dreams a reality.

Mental attitude is the theme of your thoughts, the way you describe your life, and the way you use your brain to think and interpret your experiences. Unless analyzed and reconditioned, your mental attitude is based on early childhood conditioning. This conditioning comes from the way those around you spoke to you and about you, creating a set of core beliefs. This conditioning is where you developed your internal dialogue and learned about your self-worth.

Imagine the different mental attitudes developed by the children in the following example. One child was raised in an environment with critical parents; they never acknowledged positive experiences and focused only on the child's missteps. The other child's parents gave high fives for the positive experiences and never fixated on the bad experiences.

What would you say about each child's outlook on life? What life lessons did they learn? As adults, how different are their outlooks about the world they live in? When observing other people's lives, these answers are pretty obvious, I'm sure. Yet, we do not always look into our own lives and analyze how our own core beliefs are affecting how we behave in life. We often do not consider that our beliefs are learned without our conscious acceptance, or the possibility that they can be changed.

The good news: you now have a choice. Your interactions do not have to be as they have been in the past. You have control over your mental attitude. In fact, your mental attitude is the only thing you can control. You have no real authority on how others behave or how they will react to you. But you do control how you frame things in your head, your reaction to life, and, without a doubt, your outlook on life. The sooner you accept that you cannot control every detail, the sooner you can use your mental energy on things within your control. This includes your mental attitude and, consequently, your reaction to life experiences.

The tone of your inner dialogue and how you frame conversations in your mind must matter to you. When you make room for new ways of thinking, a whole new world opens up. In my mid-twenties , I moved to Orange County, California. By the time I found a place to live and landed a job, I had no money left. I could not buy a car. So I used the not-so-efficient bus system and a bicycle way too small for my six-foot-three frame. I spent four hours commuting every day to and from work. To be at work by nine o'clock, I had to leave my apartment at six fifteen, ride my bike thirty-five minutes, and then catch a ninety-minute bus ride. This was before the luxury of iPhones and MP3s.

So instead, I devoured all the Brian Tracy books and tapes I could check out from the library. In one of his programs, he suggested writing personal affirmations and repeating them aloud until a belief was formed.

One especially cold and rainy morning, I was leaving for work on my bike. As always, I left in the dark before sunrise. The eeriness of the dark, cold, rainy morning certainly set the scene for my breakdown. I was chilled to the bone from the pouring rain, yet I was sweating underneath my raincoat. The irony of it all was too much. I began to cry. With tears running down my already wet face, I was saying, "I like myself, I like myself, I like myself," but not believing a word of it. I hated everything about what I was going through; the feeling of hopelessness was overwhelming. I remember thinking how California is the land of dreams, but I am living a nightmare. The land of the rich and beautiful people, and here I am without a bed to sleep in. I remember screaming "I hate you God!" as I pedaled my way up Brookhurst Boulevard. At that moment, something shifted. Maybe I had read enough self-help books that some of them were seeping in. I wanted things to change more than I wanted them to stay the same. I realized I had a choice. I was not a victim of my circumstances.

I shifted my focus to what I did have instead of what I did not. I was living in (usually) sunny California, where people from around the world only dreamed of living. Here I was, a kid who grew up in a small town in Turkey to living the California lifestyle. I felt some relief. Remembering my belief that everything happens for a reason, I trusted this experience was somehow benefiting me. Although the rain did not stop and I still had to catch that bus, my internal story had shifted. I started to like myself. I knew in my heart that my life was changing, my mind was changing. I did not have the words for it at the time, but my mental attitude was changing. I am sure that you have had such experiences in your life. This is how we consciously change our mental attitude.

To develop a positive mental attitude, you must commit to forming the habit. To turn a positive mental attitude into a habit, it first has to matter to you. If someone you do not know calls you and says, "I just want you to know I will never speak to you again," you would most likely say, "Okay, no problem." But if someone you deeply cared about said, "I will never speak to you again," you would definitely have a different reaction. Start by caring about your internal conversation, and how you are thinking about a subject. It is not about "efforting" to be positive or putting a smiley face sticker on an empty gas gauge. It is as simple as replaying events in your head and seeing them from a more positive perspective. Your brain in no time will take its cues from you and begin shifting how it reports and replays things, which in turn will shift how you feel about the experiences in your life.

It is nice to be in control of our reactions. Projecting positivity is even better. We are the one who is setting our own tone. Imagine you are about to walk into a meeting: if your attitude walking in is that these people are a bunch of idiots and the meeting is a total waste of time, there is a good chance you will confirm your expectations and get nothing valuable from the meeting.

Now imagine walking into the same boring corporate meeting. Before walking in, you decide to have a positive mental attitude. Say to yourself, "I'm going to be here for the next hour anyway, so let's hammer this thing out. Let me learn what others are thinking so that we can build some synergy and crank out what we need to crank out." If you were to walk into the meeting like that, I bet the experience would be vastly more rewarding. When I discovered this, my career skyrocketed. But do not take my word for it, test it out for yourself the next meeting you attend. (This works amazingly in family gatherings too.)

If you have a mental attitude that life is unfair, or people always take advantage of you, you will react to life a certain way. Naturally your interactions with those around you will reflect those beliefs. Your actions will be more guarded, and you will always look for the angle where others are trying to take advantage of you. As you can imagine, your distrusting nature will invite others to distrust you.

On the other hand, if you believe life is what you make of it and decide to trust your own abilities, even if others try to take advantage of you, you will have a different experience. When you stop playing the victim, you now control your life—you become responsible for everything that happens. Interactions with those around you become more purposeful. You interact with people differently. You become more confident, and when others feel your confidence, they are at ease as a result. The only difference is you taking charge of how you replay the stories inside your head and deciding to view life through a different filter. I am here to tell you that the filter you choose is a habit.

Because I grew up being constantly judged and corrected, I became an adult with a defensive attitude towards anyone who corrected me. A friendly reminder at work to "make sure to send that email before you leave" would sound like "Hey loser, do not be so stupid and fail to send that email." Because I was being defensive, every time someone gave me anything that resembled disapproving feedback, I denied myself the chance of improvement. When I learned it was not what others said that was annoying, but it was the filter I chose to listen through, instead of getting defensive, I started asking myself if there was another way I could look at this. Can I somehow see the benefits of this interaction and come up with a positive theme instead? By simply becoming aware of my internal dialogue, I began telling a more effective story inside my head. I became open to another way of looking at my experiences; then, the way I filtered my perceptions changed. That was the missing link that catapulted me to success.

As I shared in the introduction, I have studied an array of teachers in the self-help arena. I have no idea the number of seminars I have attended nor the amount of money I have spent on books, CDs, videos, and so on. If there was self-help stock, I would be its number one buyer. All of these books and trainings had one thing in common for me: they worked for a while, but had no lasting effect. My old habits would slowly creep back in, even though I wrote "I" statement goals in present tense, and read them morning, afternoon, and night, and created beautiful vision boards (collages of images of all the things I want to manifest in my life) and hung them in my room. Although I posted positive messages all over my walls, mirrors, and screens; used positive affirming words as my passwords; and literally repeated my positive sounding mantras thousands of times a day, the changes would not stick. I did not realize that I was putting a Band-Aid of positive talk on top of my core belief: it will not work for me.

I had no idea that I was ignoring my inner dialogue and that is why I was not getting lasting results. Regardless of the external actions I was taking, internally I was saying, "Meh! that is probably BS. I'll do these things, but it probably will not work for me." I was unaware that this was my belief system, and that my brain was working to ensure my core beliefs remained.

Because I was not paying attention to my mental attitude, none of my actions could penetrate my subconscious mind. Maybe I was conditioned to believe I was not good enough. I believed others could be successful, but I did not believe it for myself. Even when I saw others successfully using the tools I had just learned, instead of giving me hope, it instead reinforced my belief that I am not worthy. But once I recognized my mental attitude was preventing me from success, my inner dialogue started to matter to me, and I began proactively telling myself a more positive story. From there my life took off; it completely turned around.

Although the external results will not manifest overnight, your brain will continue to turn anything you repeatedly do into a habit. Your brain loves to think, think, think. It is designed for this. Just tell your brain that your internal dialogue is important to you, and you want to have a positive story inside your head. Your brain will love it. Within days, your brain will start seeing things that will be helpful to you. You will hear song lyrics answering questions you asked just a few days ago. You will get clarity about something that was troubling you while you are walking your dog. The key is to start slow and keep it light. Pay attention to your mental attitude and be curious about improving the overall theme of the story playing in your head.

Reaching any worthy goal will require action. Regardless of the area of your life, if you want to have something you do not possess, you will have to take actions to turn those dreams into realities. If you have the habit of a positive mental attitude, everything will come to you faster and you will live your life with greater ease.

Once you accept where you are in your life, and remember that all actions you take are within the boundaries of your belief system, you become more resourceful. It is definitely easier to have a positive mental attitude when it matters to you. If you can simply care about your mental attitude today and decide to tell yourself a more positive story, you will begin carving a new path for your future, a future based on your own dreams, a future based on your true calling. You must decide to take responsibility for your own mental attitude. When you consciously choose to have a positive mental attitude, your brain will notice this as something you do regularly and it will turn it into a habit. Based on my experience, once you turn your positive mental attitude into a habit, the rest comes so much easier.

Here is an exercise for the rest of this month: commit to being selfish. Decide to be selfish enough to have a positive mental attitude. Commit to being "That guy!", stubbornly focusing on maintaining a positive mental attitude.

For example, if you are running low on cash. Instead of spending your day worrying about money, which will be of no use whatsoever, tell yourself that you know how to earn more money. Remind yourself the economy goes up and down. Accept that you may be down now, but you know you can and will be up again. Do not take pretend action, but use your brain to look at your abilities to make money with a positive mental attitude.

If you are dealing with health issues, talking about your illness does not help you heal any faster. Instead think and talk to yourself about how your body is a self-healing organism. Remind yourself that even when you get a paper cut, you do not have to tell your body to heal your hand, it does it automatically. Remind yourself that there are millions of people who survived situations doctors declared terminal.

If you feel trapped in a dead end job, complaining and telling everyone how you hate your employer or colleagues does not help you get a new job. But have the mental attitude that you want to learn all you can in this job so that you can make yourself more valuable for the next job. Remind yourself there are employers somewhere looking for someone with your experience right now. Just because you have not made the connection at the moment, does not mean you will never make it.

(One word of caution here: unless people ask you what your magic formula is, try not to tell everyone what you are doing. Fight the urge to change the people around you. Work on your own mental attitude and let others find their own guide to happiness. You be selfishly you, and let others be selfishly themselves.)

CHAPTER: 5

DISCOVERING YOUR DEEP BELIEFS

Until you make the unconscious conscious, it will direct your life and you will call it fate.

–C.G. Jung

If you want to know what you truly believe in any part of your life, look at what you have created so far in that area and pay attention to how you feel about it. As we covered in the last chapter, the first step is to pay attention to your inner dialogue. Notice the *theme* of the stories you tell yourself, and the tone of the dialogue you have on any subject that matters to you. Look at the mental pictures you imagine and the words you use to describe your life experiences. For example, when you talk about your desires, do you use the language of expecting or a generally doubtful tone? When you think about your work day, do you think of self-expression and creativity or the same old crap just a different day? When making plans, do you see a successful outcome or are your plans made to prevent failure?

We have a variety of self-beliefs around the many facets of our lives. The same is true about your mental conditioning. Since we only act within the boundaries of our belief systems, you should consider your conditioned beliefs in the areas of life that are important to you. You may believe that you are a great driver, a top employee, a so-so athlete, and a terrible money manager. Some or all of those beliefs may be accurately describing where you are today, and by consciously updating your beliefs in each area, you get to create new heights for yourself. Start with general beliefs then move to specific beliefs as you get the hang of things.

Another good indication of your general mental attitude is the conversations you have with people around you. Remember, even when you are not participating in their conversations, your brain is processing the information you overhear and sends the messages to your subconscious mind. If you are around people constantly nagging about the horrible weather, crappy drivers, and annoying colleagues, it may be harder to have a positive outlook than if you are surrounded by people who are supportive and look positively at life.

When I was growing up, money consumed everyone I knew. Every decision always started with the question, "Can we afford it?" Without ever being told directly, I was conditioned with the belief system of scarcity. I learned quickly that we could not afford it because money did not grow on trees. So, to not upset people around me or make them sad, I stopped wanting.

Once I was unconsciously conditioned with the scarcity mindset, every decision I made first passed through the "Can I afford it?" filter. When scarcity is your reality, to protect yourself from feeling hurt, you begin to want less. You start settling for things rather than making bold decisions. As an adult, when I wanted to start my own business, the loop that played inside my mind was "I cannot afford to risk losing income." So I stayed unhappily working for others for many years. I hated not being able to do my own thing. I resented those who were living the life I wanted to live. To soothe my inner pain, I made up stories as to why things were working out for others and not me. This unfortunately became a self-fulfilling prophecy.

Think about the possible beliefs you were exposed to when you were a toddler. Did you experience conversations of abundance and confidence around money? Did you receive what you asked for or did you mostly hear money does not grow on trees? Were people around you loving towards others or were there conversations about how you needed to protect yourself from certain people? Just as there are no limits to our imaginations, there are also no limits to how many beliefs we can have about the different aspects of our lives. Those conversations we were exposed to about money, relationships, health, or work as children directly impact our beliefs about how successful we will be—and can be—as adults.

Once I understood the correlation between my core beliefs and my goals, I started exploring my own reality about money. One of the most eye opening things I did was to ask my mom why we were not rich. She answered that people like us do not get rich: we are honest people.

Undoubtedly, her belief about money and rich people shaped her own life experience, even if she was not consciously aware of it. Needless to say, my initial core beliefs about money, abundance, and wealth, along with my attitude towards money, were based on my subconscious observation of a twenty-five-year-old single mother who thought rich people were dishonest.

Pay attention to the stories you have on repeat. When you tune into your inner dialogue, you quickly see that there are belief loops playing in your head about any given subject (people are . . . relationships are . . . money is . . .). Continue along the same lines with any subject and you will find beliefs on a continuous loop in your brain. Once your brain accepts an idea as truth, all it is working to do is prove it right. Your brain continually looks for evidence of what you deem to be true. Your initial goal is to make sure all of your beliefs are yours because you truly believe them, not just because it is something you learned from your parents or others many years ago.

There are those who have a nagging narrative of *shoulds*. How the kids should be, how the government should run, how people should work, and how their spouse should do things differently. They should, should, should all over the place.

If you grew up in a judgmental or critical home environment, you may be someone who is conditioned to be critical of everything and everyone. You may find yourself starting conversations on a positive note, but then habitually directing the conversation to how a certain situation should be. If it is truly a conversation on self-improvement, go for it. But if it is coming from complaint, take another look. Many corporations do this by never being satisfied, thinking their people will get complacent if they say things are good. This can lead to dissatisfaction and lack of fulfillment in a business rather than boosting creativity. If you catch yourself often thinking and talking about how things around you should be, know that that is a defense mechanism against dealing with issues that make you feel powerless. Thankfully, you can consciously replace this habit of mental nagging with positive thoughts and actions that serve you better.

For many years the blaming narrative defined me. The mindset blames shortcomings on external factors: I do not have enough money because I was raised in a poor family; I cannot get a good job because I did not go to college; I cannot be successful because I did not have successful role models. This mindset essentially was an excuse I could hide behind. So instead of working on myself, I could just blame situations I felt I had no control over. This allowed me to at least think I did not have to take responsibility for my own success. I also easily recruited others to support my excuse of blaming external circumstances on my unfulfilled life. All I had to do was start throwing blame around, and quickly people agreed with me, adding fire to my beliefs.

By simply listening to your inner dialogue, there is no limit to what you can learn about yourself. Changing your mental attitude becomes easy when you can achieve a level of detached introspection.

My suggestion is to accept where you are. If you can become aware of your emotions and begin to notice the difference between positive and negative feelings, you will do fine. Whenever you are figuring out where you are, do your best not to judge. And if you find yourself judging, notice that too. It is certainly another belief you have about yourself. Do not try to jump straight into fixing yourself while you are discovering where you are. Remember awareness and acceptance are the first steps to change. The more you push against where you are, the harder it will be to change. But when you find that place of acceptance, you will discover how easily things begin to shift.

Getting down on yourself is a normal reaction when you first become aware that your own beliefs are what have been holding you back. As the saying goes, "You don't know what you don't know." Do not waste time beating up on yourself. Just take comfort in knowing every belief made sense and served you in some positive way at one point in your life. If they did not serve you in some way, they would not become a belief. You are where you are, and in the next chapter we will start shifting things. For now, continue discovering your belief system so that you can allow space for new thoughts and experiences. There is no upside to blaming your past nor to using your past as an excuse to beat up on yourself. The goal of this game is to discover your current beliefs in the areas of your life that are important to you.

What worked for me in the beginning, and what I suggest for you, is to look at one area of your life for a week and make a thorough list of your beliefs in that area before moving on to the next area. I first started with my global beliefs. What were my beliefs about life, God, the universe? Then I moved to more and more specific areas, such as career, my body, and relationships.

While discovering my inner dialogue and my core beliefs around my procrastination, I discovered that one of the reasons why I was not acting on my dreams was that I was afraid of authority figures. As a result I did not ask for what I wanted from those I deemed as authority. I was too afraid to speak and be seen. While serving in the United States Air Force, I had accumulated vacation time and had to use these days or lose them. My station captain liked me enough to call me "son," and he had always been pleasant to me. I had no external reason to be nervous. But I simply was not able to go to his office and request the time off I had earned. I stood in the hallway, pacing back and forth, palms sweaty, not able to get enough air into my lungs to speak. I pictured myself standing there in front of my captain asking for the time off. All I could envision was him jumping over his desk, attacking me for daring to ask for such a thing. It sounds crazy, I know. But that is exactly what was happening in my mind.

When I began my own journey of looking into my core beliefs, I recognized the belief about authority figures stemmed from my school days where I had a violent teacher who had beaten me. Early childhood programming is very powerful, and it cuts right through all the experiences that come after. Even after years had passed, moving thousands of miles away, and even becoming a decorated firefighter in the U.S. Air Force, in one moment I returned to the helpless child, scared and frozen by my memories of and beliefs about people in power positions. A reactionary belief to protect myself as an eight-year-old caused many occasions in my life where I could not ask for what I wanted nor share my opinions for fear of getting into trouble.

Notice which areas you are short changing yourself because of early childhood programming. Are you scared to show up to work like the person who deserves the promotion, because when you were a child, someone told you that you cannot do anything right? Are there things you need from your partner, but you are too afraid to ask because you fear abandonment? Do you keep telling yourself you are not organized enough because you were told a thousand times that you are too messy when you were a child?

To reach different results, to end up where you want to be rather than where your old programming is directing you to go, first do not dwell in your past story. Also, be careful not to justify your shortcomings by using your past as an excuse. Simply recognize the beliefs, analyze them with the knowledge you now know, and move on. If it is big stuff, do not hesitate to go to therapy, or whatever works best for you. Just be sure to have the willingness to heal and move forward. We do not want to stay stuck in our past.

We often know what it is we do not want. This is the most opportune time to ask ourselves what it is we do want. Be open to the clarity you may find about your desires while you are dealing with your past beliefs. As soon as you pay attention to your inner dialogue, you will have the awareness of where you are now. Hopefully, you have also moved into the acceptance phase. It is time to decide what you want and move in that direction.

Check your current beliefs to see where you are. Obviously quite a lot of your beliefs are going to be valid and still serve you well. You will also discover that there are many beliefs that are not moving you towards what you want. Notice them, and once you discover and accept these beliefs as something that no longer serves you, you will immediately have clarity about what you want instead.

In the next chapter, I will show you how to replace old mental attitudes with new ones. I like to move fast. If you are ready to make massive changes quickly, I suggest we leave all this baggage we brought with us here. If you need permission, this is your permission slip to be wherever you are as you are. You can leave all the junk that you have collected over the years here. Give yourself permission to see your experiences as lessons. Take the lessons and let us reset and get to the good stuff.

I'll meet you on the next page

CHAPTER: 6

SHIFTING OLD BELIEF PATTERNS

We can't be afraid of change. You may feel very secure in the pond that you are in, but if you never venture out of it, you will never know that there is such a thing as an ocean, a sea. Holding onto something that is good for you now, may be the very reason why you don't have something better.

–C. JoyBell C.

If you want to live your dream life, become proficient at shifting your mental attitude. Mastering this skill catapults your internal and external world to the next level. Shifting your mental attitude can be easy with the right guidance. Our brain turns these shifting actions into habits so that our new way of thinking and being in the world becomes automatic. All it takes is a little practice. As you know from the last chapter, whenever you are in the middle of what is unwanted, you are most clear about what it is you do want. We are going to look directly at what is holding you back, learning to interrupt the pattern and using it to your benefit.

In order to have a permanent shift in your life, you first have to ask yourself if you are willing to make a change. Many people say they want to change their mental attitude and be more positive, but they are not willing to do the work. Once you are willing and committed to shifting your mental attitude, replacing old beliefs with new ones becomes simple.

The easiest way to start shifting your mental attitude is to first work on catching yourself when you are in an unwanted frame of mind. It is impossible to monitor every thought your brain is thinking (believe me, I have tried). Instead of driving yourself crazy policing your mind, the surest way to discover your early childhood conditioning that is not serving you is to catch yourself in the middle of a breakdown. This may not seem like the time you would think is appropriate, but if you can take a breath and be calm, cool, and collected, you will discover it is actually the perfect time to notice the problem belief. Just note the experience with detachment and your reaction to it. Observe yourself from a detached place as you are perhaps having a full blown meltdown, identifying you are out of control in this area of your life.

This happened to me when in the military and I had to turn off the engines of a stealth fighter bomber plane fully loaded with bombs. In those moments of feeling out of control and like this really could be it for me, I was able to realize what I was feeling and find clarity to do the job I was assigned to do. Admitting you are out of control gives your mind space to reevaluate your situation. Let me also assure you that evaluating your existing beliefs will not be as drastic as being a firefighter in a war zone. When you catch yourself with a belief that is no longer serving you, you will want to interrupt the unwanted stream of beliefs however you can.

There are various ways to interrupt a belief pattern. I have tried tools such as snapping a rubber band around my wrist or washing my hands up to my elbows with cold water while humming the happy birthday song. But my favorite tool is a movie line from *Apollo 13* that has worked wonders for me: I say out loud, "Houston, I have a problem," whenever I catch myself in a belief stream I do not want to continue. You can use this line or any other that works for you.

Like many who received corporal punishment as a child, I had a problem regulating my anger. Often, my anger manifested itself while I was driving. Whenever I got stuck in traffic, my road rage would activate and in an instant I hated everyone around me. If someone was going too slow, he was an idiot. If someone was going too fast, she was a lunatic. If the car in front of me changed lanes or did not change lanes, I was annoyed. My anger was not about them, it was just where I was mentally. So in the middle of complete blackout road rage I yelled out loud, "Houston, I have a problem! I am in the middle of full blown road rage right now and hating life and all the people around me!"

Saying it out loud immediately weakened my anger and provided me with the space to decide on a new option. I now had the brain power to come up with how I really wanted to feel and think, instead of reacting to what I could not control. What I really wanted instead was to be unaffected by other drivers. I want to be a peaceful driver and have a nice drive to work.

By consciously disengaging your pre-existing conditioning over and over, in a very short time you will trigger your brain to turn this action into a habit, which will then become your new way of being without needing to think about it.

Let's say you have money problems and are feeling freaked out. It is normal for your brain to race out of control. After all, money is like air or food: when you do not have enough, it occupies essentially all of your thoughts. If you have money problems, there is a good chance all you think about is your lack of money. Before you know it, your brain is painting pictures of losing your house and becoming homeless. You can almost hear your loved ones ask, "Why? Why did you ever start that business, buy that house, that car, those clothes?" You may be feeling shame. Feeling like a failure. When this happens, say out loud, "Houston, I have a problem. I am freaking out about money. I am telling myself stories I do not want to tell myself. I am seeing myself powerless. I am imagining negative things and going to that dark place." By doing this it will help you separate from your conditioning around money and success. Now you can shift your thinking and start painting the image of what you do want instead. Say out loud, "I want to tell a story of abundance. I want to have lots of money. I want to feel like I have made it." And then say, "I am abundant. I do have lots of money. I have made it!"

Regardless of the size or duration of the issue, you can use this same tool every time you find yourself in the middle of an unwanted situation. Imagine you are in the middle of the "I hate my job" thought stream, thinking your boss does not appreciate you and you are underpaid for all the crap you have to deal with every day. Day in and day out your coworkers drive you crazy, and if you did not have bills, you would tell them to kiss your ass. Every day that you clock in, part of your soul breaks . . .

Just say out loud, "Houston, I have a problem! I am telling the story of a helpless person as if this is the only job left in the whole country. I want to tell the story of a person who loves his job, to see my coworkers as people who are doing their best, to feel appreciated and be paid well."

When you catch yourself in the middle of something you do not want, you have the opportunity to witness the belief that is on repeat in your brain. By inserting new ideas about what you want, you give your brain another track to loop on. Think of it like giving a thumbs down on a song you do not like and skipping to a new song you like better. The process will eventually create a playlist that will only play the songs you like best. In fact, if you can maintain a playful attitude throughout the whole process, change will happen more quickly, and you will be happier.

Do not beat yourself up over making mistakes or getting overwhelmed. That is normal. Especially when you first start paying attention to your thought processes, expect to be doing a lot of interrupting. Go for progress, not perfection. Just remember that learning to shift your mental attitude is just like learning to walk. At first it feels like effort, but once you get the hang of it, you will not even give it a second thought. And just as you do not say "get up, you little dummy" to a child who is learning to walk every time he falls down, be sure to take it easy on yourself too.

Once you start shifting your mental attitude on one subject, you can then proactively use the same skills on all aspects of your life, without waiting until disaster strikes. I wanted to earn more money. I thought about my true beliefs regarding money. I analyzed everything I believed about money for one whole day, without judgement. I discovered that, to me, money meant freedom and that the more money I made, the more freedom I would experience. This sounds like an accurate and positive statement about money. But it also reveals a belief that the only way for me to feel free is to have an abundance of money, and without having lots of money I would not be free.

"Houston, I have a problem. I do not believe I can be free without money. But I want to feel, without a doubt, that I am worthy of great things. I want to know I am always cared for. I want to believe I deserve good things." That is it. That is a better belief.

Here is another time I was curious about why I was not rich: I saw people with more money who were not as educated, well-read, or hardworking as myself. I had accepted that because they are rich and I am not, there must be something I am doing wrong. So I spent the whole weekend thinking about what I thought about rich people. I learned that I believed they were greedy. I recognized that I believed once you become rich you become a target. You had to cheat to become wealthy. "Houston, I have a problem. On one side, I want to be rich, and on the other side, I believe rich people are greedy cheaters and they suck. I want to believe that money gives you power, which you can use for good in the world. I want to feel rich and prosperous. I want to be known as the good rich guy." Since that time, I have practiced different versions of these belief-shifting games over the years.

There is not a perfect magic word; a simple break in the stream of your beliefs for you to shift is all you are going for. Some subjects may be so hairy you might not be able to go from negative to completely positive. That is okay. If there is someone you just cannot forgive for hurting you in a profound way, then gently recall the memory and listen to the words you're telling yourself and try to adjust the story from being told from the victim's perspective to a detached observer's point of view. Once you have enough material to get an idea about where you are, shift to a new belief on that subject. It could just be that you are grateful that it is over. It really is a matter of choosing. Choosing to allow a different thought into your mind.

If you want to take your shifting game to the professional athlete level, start naming both the attitude you are trying to shift and the new attitude you want instead. Essentially, creating a shorthand version. I called the part of me that was quick to anger "Postal Turk" and the part I wanted to be more active in my daily life "Cool Turk." So whenever I caught myself under the influence of Postal Turk, I would say, "Houston, I have a problem. Postal Turk took control and is making my life a living hell. I request Cool Turk to take charge of this situation." Or if I was getting apprehensive before a meeting, where my mind was going through all the reasons why things were not going to work out, I would quickly request that I could use some of Cool Turk's influence right now. (Recall the bus driver analogy from chapter one.)

If you are hoping you will turn from a totally negative person to a totally positive person by playing the shift game one time, you are fooling yourself. Yes, you may decide to be more positive, but as I explained in the first part of the book: all habits take time. To ensure you will not be discouraged after the first five times, turn changing your mental attitude into a game. Rather than worrying about and getting overwhelmed, see how many times you can shift to something more positive in a day. Then, on the next day, see if you can shift more thoughts than you did the day before. Go for incremental increases, and celebrate along the way.

Having a positive mental attitude is the number one habit. But it is not going to stop there. You will still have to build other habits. You will have to take actions where you will be uncomfortable. But once you learn to control your mental attitude, you will become the master of your interpretation of events and circumstances, and you will be able to extract more from your day to day life. This is why mastery of one's mental attitude is the greatest skill and the number one habit everyone should work on attaining.

CHAPTER: 7

HOW TO ACHIEVE MASTERY

An expert is not a university educated professor, it is a person that has demonstrated mastery of the subject through practical experience, excellent results and numerous highly rated publications.

–Steven Magee

A positive mental attitude is not like getting a college degree: you cannot claim mastery of a positive mental attitude because you achieved it once and assume you are good to go for the rest of your life; it is more of a skill you learn. Just like with any new skill, it feels awkward at first, but once you learn, you will likely always remember how to do it, just like riding a bike. But only those who take the time and energy to practice become masters. When we watch any master in their field, whether an athlete like Serena Williams, a musician like Yo-Yo Ma, or a chef like Gordon Ramsey, you clearly see they have gained their respected positions by focusing and working longer than anyone else on perfecting their skills. When you listen to a master's story, you hear how they learned from their failures, moved forward, and continually committed themselves to give their best every time. I know this is a tall order. In fact, that is why although many people want to become a master in their field, very few commit to the work it requires to achieve the goal. I often have better command of the English language I learned as a second language than many native English speakers because I committed myself to it.

Great news! Unlike a sport or instrument, the work to master your mental attitude takes place inside your head and requires absolutely no exertion. Just like your physical body, your brain also needs certain daily exercise. And believe me, you will have plenty of opportunities to exercise this new habit. Afterall, life happens to all of us. Someone will do you wrong, throw you under the bus, or accuse you of something you did not do. You may experience dark days, weeks, or even months where you cannot see the bright side of your experiences. But once you decide to control your mental attitude, you will always find your way back to the light. Mastery of a positive mental attitude only requires a decision to take the time to look at life's happenings from a positive perspective. Nothing more.

To master your mental attitude, first you have to shed the burdens holding you back. The first step to lightening your load is to forgive. When you are able to forgive those you feel have wronged you, you will progress at high speed. This, of course, includes forgiving yourself—our parents too.

When I first heard the idea of forgiving others to free myself from the bondage of my past, I simply did not accept the notion. I believed there was no way to forgive or forget the fear and mental anguish of physical and emotional abuse and abandonment I lived. I learned forgiveness is not about righting the wrongs, and it does not mean you have to like the person or are now okay with what you experienced. It is not about forgetting or pretending it did not happen. By forgiving, you are removing the emotional charge and grip the person or incident has on you. It is about you becoming free of the old chains that have been holding you back.

Forgiving an abusive ex-partner does not make the abuse acceptable. It does not magically turn the ex-partner into a nice person. But it may shine light on why you are not able to speak up. You now might be able to comprehend why you are uneasy in certain situations. Forgiveness provides you with the mental room to shift your beliefs by accepting that being afraid in particular situations is okay, and, in turn, it empowers you.

The second secret of positive-mental-attitude mastery is selfishness. Now, I'm not talking about being selfish and hurting others; I am talking about being selfish enough to care about how you feel, that you make sure that your peace of mind is what matters to you most. We have no control over how others react to us, what others think of our actions, or what problems may be waiting for us around the corner. You are human and in the process of living; lousy things are going to happen to you and around you. But if you insist that your peace of mind is your top priority, your brain will experience these events in a way that serves you.

The best time to practice positive thinking is when things are going well. On a good day, notice the little annoyances and see if you can shift your perspective. Practice choosing a new perspective and notice what there is to learn in that situation. Then, when the lousy experiences occur, the habit will have been put into place, and you will easily access your positive mental attitude.

You may be right in blaming your upbringing for the problems you have with authority figures. You can claim you are codependent because of your childhood. You may have shortcomings because of traumas you experienced. All of those statements may be true and valid. But giving up your current power to your past will deny you the opportunity to take ownership of those experiences, making you a slave to old circumstances rather than the master of your life. Just decide. Decide to be selfish enough to care about how you feel, to refuse to feel sorry for yourself, and to think about anything and everything you do with a lighthearted, positive spin. Do not merely try to be positive. Actually decide to be a positive person, and do things with a positive mental attitude. Walk your talk like you mean it .

The third practice to mastering your mental attitude is reframing (i.e., claiming responsibility). When you take responsibility for the meaning you attach to an experience, you immediately rise above the present circumstance. You become the narrator of your life rather than a character in a story you did not author.

In the morning, before involving anyone else, whether it be your partner, your dog, or your Starbucks barista, make the preemptive decision to expand how you experience each moment. You will notice right away how your day becomes full of new choices and possibilities; however, remember just as easily, if you decide the day sucks already, there is a good chance you will find evidence of that as well.

It is nice when our day goes as planned and the positive vibes come easily. But, when we are caught up in horrific circumstances, if we have practiced our positive mental attitude consistently, we are able to access it in the most extreme of cases.

I was acquainted with a political prisoner who was tortured for three weeks while in jail. One night after a few drinks she shared her story of all the unspeakable acts she experienced while in police custody. I was cringing in pain as if I was the one being hung, shocked, and beaten until I lost consciousness. Just hearing what she had to endure made me want to throw up. When I asked her how she did it, her answer was simple: she had refused to let the officer break her spirit. She simply decided that her current situation was indeed the most horrifying moments of her life, and she knew that nothing after this would ever be as monstrous. Her mind was determined to stay strong and survive the encounter. And indeed, she did.

I am grateful to have never experienced such an extreme situation. But it goes to show you that when you make up your mind about who you are and what you are about, even the people who are seemingly controlling your life, and even the prospect of death, become powerless.

The most efficient and effective way to master an unshakeable positive mental attitude is through meditation. As you probably noticed, there is no shortage of spokespeople for meditation—that is because meditation works. I follow the suggestion of my favorite spiritual teacher, Abraham, and practice meditation first thing in the morning for fifteen to twenty minutes. It is simple and it works for me.

There are many ways to meditate. You can sit in silence, meditate in groups, or use apps on your phone. As long as you can spend quiet time listening to your inner dialogue, that is enough. I suggest you not make it complicated. Do not make it into something it is not. Meditation is you sitting quietly and listening to your inner guidance. Done!

Your ability to quiet your mind will allow you to know how mental silence feels, when there are no screens, ads, or likes and dislikes tugging at your brain. Habituating the practice of meditation allows you to differentiate between your own inner knowing and the influences of others around you. With practice, you can easily learn to use meditation to stop the momentum of bad thinking. Whenever life gets away from me and everything is spinning out of control, when I do not know where to start, but I know things are going nuts, I excuse myself and take a few minutes to stop the momentum. Whether going into a bathroom to get centered or going for a quick walk outside, I find a place to close my eyes and just be. I do whatever I can to take two minutes to breathe and listen to my inner dialogue. This allows me to center myself where I can find a new perspective and my positive mental attitude.

Visualization is another tool to help you build habits. Visualize yourself as the master of the number one habit, your mental attitude. How would your day be different if you were consciously aware of your thinking and living with a positive mental attitude?

Purposefully intend how you want each segment of your day to go. Pave the way for a day filled with your positive perspective. This does not mean, of course, that you will not have bumps along the way. But what it does mean is that you will be able to handle those bumps in a more productive way. You will be open to learning and expanding.

In his famous book, *The 7 Habits of Highly Effective People*, Stephen Covey wrote about Benjamin Franklin's commitment to his own mental attitude by developing a list of thirteen virtues. In his pocket, Benjamin Franklin kept a piece of paper where he had written the thirteen virtues he wanted to master. Every day he kept track of his behaviors around all thirteen virtues, but he always had one main focus each week.

When I read this, I knew it was something I also wanted to do. I like working from a list, so it was natural for me to create the list of areas I wanted to work on. I wrote my list of areas, chose one, and got to work. I first gained greater awareness of where I actually stood in a particular area and what I could do to improve.

I checked my mental attitude throughout the day, but focused in the main area I wanted to master until I moved on to the next area of my life I wanted to improve. Give yourself time. Choose an area in your life you would like to work on and take a week or even a month to master it. Do your best not to stress about the process of changing or getting it right. By focusing on your positive mental attitude each day, your brain adjusts quickly to the new ways of thinking, creating your new habits and ways of being in the world. It may not sound like it is possible to change habits you have had for many years in just a few weeks, but I am here to tell you it is. Always remember, it is about progress, not perfection.

As I shared earlier, I started with the general, yet pretty expansive, areas of my life, asking myself what my concept of the Universe, or God, really is and if I have the belief that life is hard or life is easy. Then I moved on to more specific areas in my life, such as money, my diet, and my personal relationships. You can do this however works best for you. My first question was, "Do I live like I believe in a friendly, loving, benevolent God? Or do I live like I believe in a vindictive, mean God who is sitting in the sky, keeping a close eye on my screw-ups?" I realized that—although I said I believed in a loving Universe—I acted as if I believed the opposite.

So in the first thirty days, I worked on improving my understanding of God. Every time I caught myself thinking that the universe I lived in was a hostile one, I would stop and ask myself, "Which do I believe in, a friendly or a hostile universe?" Once I declared I believed in a friendly universe, it provided me with a whole new perspective. I continued this for a month. For the first couple of days, it felt like I was catching myself every few minutes. But before I knew it, I could look at something that would typically piss me off and immediately think, "I believe in a friendly universe and there is something positive that will come from this."

Then I worked on my beliefs about my own self. How did I think of myself? It became clear rather quickly my self-talk and the pictures I conjured about myself were not helpful at all. So when I caught myself internally saying that I was not good enough, lazy, or undisciplined, I would replace that talk with more soothing words, like "as long as I am willing, I can learn anything I need to learn." I asked myself, "Am I really an inferior human to others or have I been making different decisions than those people I deemed successful?" With questions like these, I was able to shift my perception and allow for new, more helpful beliefs to be formed.

At the time, I was working for a carpet cleaning company, and many of our accounts were these huge, spectacular homes on the lake. Because I had been working on my positive mental attitude around money, my habits of thinking had already started to change. One day I was standing in a home overlooking the water, admiring the boat docked nearby. The owners walked in and we began talking. I noticed my feelings of inferiority were no longer there. The shift in my mental attitude had already taken place from negative to positive about those who were rich. I was able to talk with them equal to equal. Standing there in admiration, I knew I would have my version of this one day too. My belief that all rich people were smarter than me was no longer true. I recognized that they were normal people who were doing things differently and that I could learn from doing things their way.

If I have learned anything from life so far, it is this: for those of us who want to reach worthy goals, there is never an end to the work we do on ourselves. So I suggest you take it easy. When you are continually growing and expanding, there is no shortage of areas to work on. As soon as I shifted my beliefs about money and started making money, I came face-to-face with my fear of losing it all. This is, of course, caused by a different set of programming. Mastery does not mean your work is done for good; it simply means you are enjoying the work, having fun, and always practicing— and you will make even the difficult times look easy.

True mastery comes from being present while you are practicing, incrementally improving, and being committed to learning from your mistakes. Watch anyone who is considered a master, and you will see they are hardworking but doing it with fun, ease, and grace. This is true whether you are Lebron James mastering the game of basketball, a master chef slicing an onion with perfect precision, or you yourself taking the time to master your own positive mental attitude one day at a time.

FINALLY, MAKE YOUR LIFE EASIER

> *Freedom is not the absence of commitments, but the ability to—and commit myself to choose—what is best for me.*
>
> –Paulo Coelho, **The Zahir**

The Burmese were close to invading Thailand in 1767. The nonviolent Buddhists monks living in Thailand were aware of their potential slaughter. They wanted to protect the three-hundred-year-old, ten-foot golden buddha statue in the temple they worshiped. Since they had no way of moving a five-ton statue, the monks decided to cover it with plaster and colored glass to conceal its true value. Soon after, the Burmese invaded Thailand and, as expected, killed every monk in the temple, sparing no one. Because the Burmese fighters did not bother with the plastered statue, it remained untouched for two centuries. In 1967 while moving the statue to another location, the workers accidentally dropped the statue, causing the outer layer to break away. Underneath the debris of glass and plaster shined hints of what lay beneath: a pristine and beautiful golden buddha.

I do not know the details of your life, but I do know we share a common life story that began in a similar way. We are all born as pure bundles of joy and full of potential. We were helpless and fully dependent on others for our survival. We naturally domesticated to the beliefs of the tribe that raised us. We wanted to fit in and be liked by others around us, so we accepted their beliefs as ours. There is no one who is an exception to this.

Those beliefs you accepted, without questioning, are like the plaster covering the golden Buddha, hiding your true nature and potential just below the surface.

You have been hiding long enough. It is time to peel away the plaster and let your true brightness shine. It is time for you to claim your true worth, time to go after the dreams you have been ignoring. Now is your time to shine the light that has been dimmed. True satisfaction comes from having dreams and going after them. Look at anyone who feels they are living an unfulfilled life of regret and numbness and you will see the person who did not go after their dreams.

There is no new skill needed to master your mental attitude. It can be done as quickly as today. You have access to all you need, because everything is within you already. It is far easier to reach your goals than you previously believed. You do not need another tool and you certainly do not need someone else's permission to reclaim your true power. The only adjustment required is the commitment to have a positive mental attitude, which will guarantee you live a more easeful life.

You do not need to struggle to make something of your life. You can enjoy every day of your life and become rich, have great health, have amazing friends and partners, and leave a legacy. You are not here to live a boring life. You are not designed to work all of your life just to pay bills. You are designed to create. You are meant to dream up ideas and go out and turn those dreams into reality and do it again and again and again.

I hope what I have shared here resonated with you enough so that you take the first step and peel away that protective plaster, letting your true light shine. I know you can be rich beyond your wildest dreams. I know you can have a strong, agile, and flexible body at any age. I also know you can have an amazing life partner and friends who excite and support you. All those things are possible for you and everyone else too. You can be, do, and have anything and everything you want. I know if you are at a low point in your life—like I was many times—these words may seem like a guy writing some positive sounding words to sell a book. I assure you that everything I have written in this book is based on what I have learned, tested, and applied in my own life. I have gone from being at the mercy of others to being in a place of doing only what I want, when I want. Is my work done? Never.

Work is necessary, but how we show up to work and decide to carry ourselves is entirely within our control. Take this book for example: as I am typing the final words, I cannot help but savor the moment of its completion; it takes me back to the beginning of this particular journey—the day I felt my lowest and loneliest—I had just called my landlord to tell her I did not have money to pay the rent that month, and I would be moving if I was not able to figure something out, knowing full well I had less than a dollar, no food, and absolutely nowhere to turn. On that sunny winter day, realizing at the end of the month I would literally be homeless, I could not scream loud enough, cry hard enough, or wish strong enough to change my situation.

I was at my rock bottom. In order to prevent myself from going crazy, I forced myself to think about the good things that had happened to me in my life so far. In less than fifteen minutes, although nothing externally had changed, I was not feeling sorry for myself. I began to feel better, more capable. I realized within minutes of simply guiding my brain to think purposefully, I went from thinking about the implications of becoming homeless to thinking about a day when I would become rich, and the day I would share my story in a book—this book—about my journey from rags to riches starting on that day.

I will share more of my journey in future books, but meanwhile let's stay connected. You can join the community www.thenumberonehabit.com and share your story with me.

In these final words I want to ask you to play this game with me for the next thirty days.

Small or large, before taking your next action, pause and decide for yourself the most positive way you can approach any situation. Before going into a meeting, ask yourself, "How will I show up? How can I make this a positive experience?" Before engaging with someone, ask yourself, "What are the positive aspects of this person?" Before heading into a sticky situation, think about the possibility of something positive to be gained out of this. Refuse to allow others or your situation dictate how you should be. Look at everything like a stubborn kid who wants it all her way.

Commit to playing this game for the next thirty days. If it sucks, you can always go back to your old ways at the end of it. But I know it will not.

What will happen is your true nature will come to the surface. You will start carrying yourself more positively. You will be more confident. People will respond to you differently. You will start to create such positive momentum that you will not want to go back. You will have no choice but to go after all your dreams and desires. Do not take my word for it. Test it out for yourself.

I cannot thank you enough for sharing this journey with me. If you need support, you can find it here at www. thenumberonehabit.com. I hope you stay in touch and share your success stories with me.

REFERENCES

Covey, Stephen R. 1989. *The 7 Habits of Highly Effective People: Powerful Lessons in Personal Change*. New York: Simon & Schuster.

About the Author

Turk Akbay is a seeker, author, inspirational speaker, consultant, and most of all, an uplifter.

He immigrated to the United States as a teenager in search of living the American dream. Turk has dedicated over thirty years of his life to his own personal development and, in turn, to helping others reach their full potential by self-actualizing their own greatness.

Turk has a natural gift of viewing and experiencing life, and as a speaker, he expresses life in ways that bring his audience into new perspectives. He easily conveys high-level thinking in a light and humorous way.

As an author, he views his writings as co-creative experiences with his reader. He challenges their beliefs by exploring new thought ideas, allowing his readers to discover for themselves their own truth. Readers are left with a new awareness and appreciation for life and are inspired to reach for more of the life they desire.

Turk Akbay is a decorated veteran of the U.S. Air Force. He is the inventor of Subliminal Coaching, a patented system of reprogramming one's subconscious mind from sabotaging to empowering. He is the founder and co-founder of multiple companies and a TEDx Speaker; the talk can be found on YouTube and is titled "Are you 'Being' an American?"

For more information, visit www.turkakbay.com.

www.ingramcontent.com/pod-product-compliance
Lightning Source LLC
Chambersburg PA
CBHW031537040426
42445CB00010B/576